YES, BUT...

THE TOP 40 KILLER PHRASES AND HOW YOU CAN FIGHT THEM

Charles "Chic" Thompson

with

Lael Lyons

HarperBusiness
A Division of HarperCollinsPublishers

OTHER BOOKS BY CHARLES CHIC THOMPSON

What a Great Idea! (1992)

HarperCollins books may be purchased for educational, business, or sales promotional use. For information please write: Special Markets Department, HarperCollins Publishers, Inc., 10 East 53rd Street, New York, NY 10022.

FIRST EDITION

Layout design: *Douglas Hamann*
Cartoon illustrations: *Stephen Burgess*

Library of Congress Cataloging-in-Publication Data

Thompson, Charles, 1948-
    Yes, but . . . : the top 40 killer phrases and how you can fight them / Charles "Chic" Thompson with Lael Lyons. – 1st ed.
        p.   cm.
    ISBN 0-88730-660-8
    1. Creative ability in business. 2. Creative ability. 3. Conflict management.
I. Lyons, Lael. II. Title.
HD53.T47 1993
658.3'14—dc20   93-39848

94 95 96 97 98   10 9 8 7 6 5 4 3 2 1

DEDICATION

To all who are inspired to venture beyond Killer Phrase boundaries, tapping the unlimited possibilities of their imaginations.

With special thanks and love to the people who continue to inspire us: our parents, Larry and Eleanor Thompson, Sam and Carol Lyons; and Lael's uncle, Keith Lyons.

ACKNOWLEDGMENTS

*YES, **BUT**...* represents the collaborative work of many creative individuals who saw an idea and made it a reality: Susan Moldow, editor-in-chief, and Nancy Peske, assistant editor, at HarperCollins; Rafe Sagalyn, literary agent; Stephen Burgess, cartoonist; Doug Hamann, graphic designer; Victoria Brookshire Dunham, Stacy Anne Soffe, and Kristina Myren Sheldon at Creative Management Group; and Robert Brown, M.D., Ph.D., cognitive psychology consultant.

The reviewers' thoughtful appraisals and clear insights helped refine existing concepts and spark better ones: Jan Allen, Catherine Avery, Chip Jones, Joan Kufrin, Sam Lyons, John Miller, Jennifer Norton, Chong Pak, and Patricia Worrell.

*YES, **BUT**...* owes its greatest thanks to people all over the world who have shared their favorite Killer Phrases, including: AlexZan, Deborah Armstrong, Bruce Blaylock, H. Bolt, Roger Britt, Laura Conrad, Thomas Costello, Tam Deachman, John deLorimier, Nancy Dubiell, Dave Dufour, David Dyson, C.J. Fayard, Leonard Fedoruk, Howard Flagler, Sal Gabbay, Susan Gaede, Andy Galloway, Jean-Louis Gassee, Scott Gassman, Bill Gordon, Joe LeGrand, Joyce Gubbins, Jerry Hamilton, Bob Harrell, Marybeth Highton, Clyde Jackson, Maureen Keresman, Clancy Kress, Sharon Letourneau, Tim LoGrasso, Posy Lough, Karl Mettke, Francie Micale, Marnie Montgomery, Paul Montgomery, Chuck Nakell, Jeff Nicholson, Laurel O'Connor, A.R. Rottenborn, Lynn Santamaria and class, Ruth Schermitzler, Linda Sharp, Paul Shorock, Ken Simendinger, Bart Simpson, Tim Smith, Rich Sojka, Justine Staub, Russ Sype, Stephanie Tomasic, Bill Wagenseller, Dan Zadra.

CONTENTS

GREAT IDEAS   Unleashing Innovation

When was the last time you had an idea but a little voice inside your head said "It'll never work" and talked you out of it? Have you ever offered a suggestion only to hear your boss bark "That's not your responsibility"? So, you just sat on your idea. Then months later someone else came up with your great idea and was rewarded for it.

> *"We tried that before."*
> *"The competition will eat you alive."*
> *"You're too young."*
> *"Yes, BUT..."*

These are Killer Phrases, nominated "America's Most Dangerous Export" by *World Trade* magazine.

> **Killer Phrase** (kĭl'ər frāz) - *n.* 1. a knee-jerk response that squelches new ideas; most commonly said by bosses, parents and government officials. 2. a threat to innovation.

We are bombarded by Killer Phrases every day. They stifle our ideas, short-circuit creative thinking and undercut the very notion of innovation. Even worse, they talk us out of our hopes and dreams.

As we discussed in *What a Great Idea!* the negative voice of "It'll never work" has been around a long time. In 1899, the Director of the U.S. Patent Office declared, "Everything has been invented," and tried to close the Office down. Now five million patents later, that voice is saying "The boss will never go for it" to employees' suggestions.

> At work, 91% of all responses to requests are negative, usually followed by "It's not in the budget" or "We've never done it that way."

> **"There's no future in believing something can't be done. The future is in making it happen."**
>
> — *TRW advertisement*

At home, our children hear an average of 432 negative statements per day, stifling their desire to find out how something works. "No... Stop... Don't touch... Don't play with that."

At school, teachers may say a dozen negative statements to every positive one, perhaps to students eager to answer or ask a question. "Be still... Don't talk... Don't do that."

Killer Phrases have been around since the dawn of time. Look at the good old reliables such as "It'll never fly." Check out today's hottest topics and you'll find today's latest Killer Phrases, for instance: "Tom Peters would never go for it" or "It doesn't meet the quality criteria." We hear Killer Phrases throughout our lives, from infancy to retirement.

Of course, we need warnings. I'd be grateful to have anyone shout, "No, don't do that!" right before I step into the path of a moving train. And when I'm trying out a new idea, I appreciate constructive feedback. Killer Phrases are different, arising from our natural resistance to change. The naysayer's goal is to stop ideas in their tracks, before they have a chance to disrupt the status quo. Killer Phrases are those uniquely negative statements that make us think, "Gee, I wish I'd never said that" and to think twice before we offer the next suggestion. The result: the average American worker now only submits one written suggestion every ten years. The average Toyota worker in Japan submits twenty-four per year.

But now, more than ever, we need great ideas. We need them to revive our economy, to restore our family, to empower our employees and to reinvent our schools. So, to give new ideas a chance, we need to understand the root cause of Killer Phrases and evolve past them.

FIGHT BACK <u>Your Winning Strategy</u>

Think about the most powerful Killer Phrases in your life, ones that strike fear and terror in your new idea's heart. I've got great news. One strategy effectively fights most Killer Phrases – even the "knee-knocking" ones.

The Fight Back model has four steps.

1. **I**dentify the Killer Phrase
2. **D**etermine the root cause
3. **E**xplore your options
4. **A**ct

When you put the steps together, they form the acronym **I.D.E.A.** Because that's the whole point – diffusing Killer Phrases to clear the way for new ideas. You can use this model to deal with the Killer Phrases people say to you, as well as the ones you say to yourself.

STEP 1: Identify the Killer Phrase

This step is short, yet awareness is the most important step you can take to overcome Killer Phrases. They are like overdue bills. Ignoring them won't make them go away. The instant you hear or anticipate a Killer Phrase, your internal voice should kick in with "Hey, that's a Killer Phrase!" and begin to deal with it.

Here's some fast help in identifying Killer Phrases:

Scan the Table of Contents.
Note the a/k/a (also known as) entries on each Killer Phrase page.
Check out the list on page 90.

You'll become instantly aware of over 250 world-class Killer Phrases.

> "We need to make the world safe for creativity and intuition, for it's creativity and intuition that will make the world safe for us."
>
> — *Edgar Mitchell,* Apollo *astronaut*

3

STEP 2: Determine the Root Cause

When you detect a Killer Phrase, your mission is to determine *why* the person is flinging a Killer Phrase at you, so you know *what* to do to overcome it.

The more you know about "why," the better equipped you will be to respond effectively. Sometimes "why" relates to your idea, sometimes to the naysayer. For example, what does this person stand to lose if your idea wins – power, security, status?

To uncover the root cause for a specific Killer Phrase, try asking why the Killer Phrase is occurring, and then counter the answer with "Why?" four more times. (See example on page 8.)

To get you started, I've organized the top 40 Killer Phrases into seven initial "why" categories. These categories draw from the trends I see in business today and from cognitive psychology, a discipline devoted to moving beyond self-defeating, negative thought patterns.

Category	When people say:	They really mean:
Catastrophizing	Do you realize the paperwork it will create?	Your idea is a huge problem.
Comparative Thinking	We've always done it THIS way.	The status quo looks better than your idea.
Overgeneralization	It'll never work!	In a win-lose world, your idea loses.
Put-downs	Don't waste time thinking.	Your idea (and perhaps you) are inferior or threatening.
Selective Editing	It's not in the budget.	Your idea doesn't survive the first cut.
Stalls	Put it in writing.	Your idea is too much, too fast.
Zero Defects	It doesn't meet our quality standards.	Your idea isn't immediately perfect.

STEP 3: Explore Your Options

Your basic plan is always to respond to the real issue. Then...

Comparative Thinking/Selective Editing: Help the naysayer *shift to a new perspective* to create an accurate comparison.

Catastrophizing/Overgeneralization/Zero Defects: Help the naysayer *put your idea into a larger context,* creating some room to maneuver and making it safe to take a manageable risk.

Put-downs/Stalls:
Get some *grassroots support* for your idea before the meeting.

STEP 4: Act

To act on your idea, you need to sell your idea. This requires a boundaryless* promotional campaign that works *in, out, up* and *down.*

Sell yourself so that your vision becomes a fire IN your belly – then radiate that energy to others. When it's time to influence a wider audience, sell OUT-side by telling family and friends, and publicizing your idea in the media. Think like your boss' boss to help your idea take wings and fly UP the organization. Change shoes with employees two levels DOWN to identify the best ways to encourage active involvement and buy-in.

The **I.D.E.A.** model works as a general strategy or in conjunction with the more specific strategies found throughout the book. Use the "Leadership Actions" to create an environment that actively welcomes new ideas.

Our first Killer Phrase is in a class by itself. "Yes, BUT..." forms the prefix to many other Killer Phrases. The next two pages will help you understand *why* managers are saying "Yes, BUT..." and *what* you can do to fight back.

> * **Boundaryless:**
> "elimination of boundaries between businesses and the transferring of ideas from one place in the Company to another."
>
> — GE Annual Report

YES, BUT...

The #1 Killer Phrase of all time. A politically correct, sweet 'n sour, little two-step that gives with one hand as it takes back with the other. "Yes, BUT..." is suitable for any occasion from international trade negotiations to selecting the right tie.

> a/k/a: Yeah, but...
>   Yahbut...
>   You're right, but...

Look beyond the "BUT" to find the true message.

Handle objections. Often "Yes, BUT..." is a prefix for additional Killer Phrases, such as "It's not in the budget" or "We tried that before." Clarify the concern – image, cost, past failure – and address it.

Be a detail person. If "Yes, BUT..." is a request for more information, provide it. Consider using examples, statistics or a demonstration to make your idea come alive for your audience.

Stay open. "Yes, BUT..." can be a dramatic way to inform or to gain attention. Use the information after "BUT" to make your idea even stronger. Work together to create an alternative solution that incorporates the new perspective.

Check it out. People frequently use this Killer Phrase as conversational filler, like "you know." If you can substitute "Yes, AND" for "Yes, BUT" – without changing the meaning – chances are it's not meant to be a Killer Phrase.

> **"Yes-AND is an agenda for action."**
>
> — *Dr. Arthur Freeman & Rose DeWolf,*
> The 10 Dumbest Mistakes Smart People Make

LEADERSHIP ACTION:

"Yes, AND" allows a dialogue. "Yes, BUT..." offers an excuse for ending the discussion. Replace "Yes, BUT..." with "Yes, AND" in your own conversations and watch the empowered response. Start an awareness campaign. Put "No *Yes, BUT's* allowed" posters around the office.

YES, BUT...

A Working Example

We've talked about two things in this section: the four-step **I.D.E.A.** process and the Killer Phrase "Yes, BUT." These work alone, or you can combine them with any of the 40 Killer Phrase pages to create customized strategies. Here's how it might work.

> Your Great Idea: "We need to upgrade our computer system."
> Naysayer's response: "Yes, BUT...we can't possibly fund it."

STEP 1: Identify the Killer Phrase

"Yes, BUT..."

STEP 2: Determine the root cause

In your mind, ask why the Killer Phrase is occurring, then counter the answer with "Why?" four more times:

Why?   Budgets are tight, so every new idea is measured solely in terms of money.
Why?   Boss was told to make 10% cut.
Why?   We lost money last quarter.
Why?   New product introduction was delayed.
Why?   Quality problem with supplier.
ROOT CAUSE: Poor quality raw materials from supplier.

STEP 3: Explore your options

Diffuse* the Killer Phrase by addressing the quality issue. Show how an upgraded computer system provides improved materials tracking and better quality control documentation.

Refer to related Killer Phrase pages, such as "It's not in the budget," on page 66, for additional strategies.

STEP 4: Act

Develop your strongest option into action items, such as a meeting with the quality control department to investigate possible cost savings.

> * **Diffuse: to divert, deflect or neutralize a Killer Phrase before it does lasting damage.**
>
> — *from* What a Great Idea!

CATASTROPHIZING

"The sky is falling." — *Chicken Little*

"My figures coincide in setting 1950 as the year that the world must go smash."
— *Henry Adams, historian, 1903*

"And they'll be Sorry." — *Eeyore in A.A. Milne's* The House at Pooh Corner, *1928*

"Good God! I can't publish this. We'd both be in jail."
— *publisher, rejecting William Faulkner's* Sanctuary *(published 1931)*

> **"Any change is scary, and when we are scared we use our power of fantasy to come up with scenarios of disaster."**
>
> — *Dr. Arthur Freeman & Rose DeWolf,* Woulda, Coulda, Shoulda

Uh-oh. Ghoulies and ghosties. Nightmares. Paranoia. Panic in the streets. Catastrophizers assume the worst, then build a case to match. Result: they are never unpleasantly surprised – or pleasantly surprised.

Granted, we need to consider potential risks and dangers. But these quintessential pessimists rush immediately to the dark side of every new idea...and stay there. Blessed are they who have low expectations for they shall not be disappointed.

The key to brightening the Catastrophizer's view is to provide a little contrast. You can add a few shades of gray to the Catastrophizer's palette thus shedding some light on your great idea.

DAVID vs. GOLIATH REVISITED

THE COMPETITION WILL EAT YOU ALIVE.

This super-efficient Killer Phrase chews up your idea and spits it out before the competition ever has a chance. With naysayers like these, who needs enemies?

> *a/k/a:* *They'll clean your clock.*
> *They'll eat your lunch.*
> *You'll never work here again.*
> *Your friends will abandon you.*

Understanding the power sources of this Killer Phrase can help transform your suggestion into the New Idea du Jour.

Absolute Zero Chance of Success. Worst case, how badly will they eat us? Best case, could we eat THEM? What happens in between? If we succeed, maybe all they'll be eating is our *dust.*

A Higher Authority. The naysayer has sacrificed personal opinion in favor of a more powerful group. Why? Do a reality check. Has the dire prediction been true in the past? What's different about this time?

Personal Attack. You're the target. Shift the attention back to the idea. Look for ways to neutralize resistance and gain support.

LEADERSHIP ACTION

Toss out a few crumbs of your idea first to find out exactly how hungry "they" are. What will it take to pacify them long enough to give your idea a chance?

Auto makers and computer manufacturers are discovering what field mice have always known: stationary targets are easy prey. So learn from nature – keep evolving, keep moving, and survive.

If you can't beat 'em, join the new global trend – a steady migration from "Never trust the competition" to "Let's form a partnership."

> "Compete by collaborating in order to avoid competing."
>
> — *Tom Peters,*
> Liberation Management

11

DO YOU REALIZE THE PAPERWORK IT WILL CREATE?

What sounds like a plea to protect the environment is probably a Killer Phrase to protect the status quo.

> a/k/a: We're all too busy.
> It'll run up overhead.
> That would be too difficult to administer.
> If I hear one more suggestion, my head will explode.

Communicate your proposal without killing trees or ideas.

Make it paperless. Promote your idea as an opportunity to redesign your paper-ridden processes. Ford Motor Company instituted invoiceless billing. Mutual Benefit Life cut their insurance application time by 60%.

Make the paper more valuable. Review your idea and eliminate "junk work." Link any remaining documentation to a specific business advantage, such as increased quality or reduced administrative time. Strengthen your case by showing how other benefits outweigh additional paperwork.

> **"Nothing is more wasteful than doing with great efficiency that which should not be done."**
>
> — *Theodore Levitt, former editor,* Harvard Business Review

LEADERSHIP ACTION

Is your organization's paper trail drowning good efforts? Try shredding the procedures rather than the idea. GE Work-Out's continuous improvement process reduces paperwork by focusing on three S's: speed, simplicity and self-confidence. GE managers had "always" needed twenty-three signatures for their new-hire process – now they do fine with eight.

YOU CAN'T FIGHT CITY HALL!

The Killer Phrase that says don't argue with omnipotence. But anyone who has watched the Wizard of Oz knows that there really is someone behind the screen.

> a/k/a: We don't have the authority.
> It's against company policy.
> Don't buck the system.
> Don't stir up the fire unless you can put out the flame.

Shift the perspective from "us vs. them" to "we, the people."

Define "fight." Is it really a fight you want? Fights are win-lose. How can you make this a win-win solution?

Redefine "City Hall." If you perceive City Hall as merely bureaucratic and power hungry, you're behind the times. Across the country and around the world, people are reinventing governments to be more responsive to individuals and more collaborative with businesses.

Get personal. Who is City Hall, anyway? The Mayor, the Chief of Police...a collection of individuals with unique perspectives. Break huge institutions into manageable chunks so you can begin to deal with each stakeholder's motivation to support your idea. Edison gained government support for his light bulb project simply by stating, "You'll be able to tax it."

LEADERSHIP ACTION

Reinvent your own organization along the lines of future-thinking governments. Rally your constituents through a collective vision and attainable goals. Provide champions and mentors for staff members willing to risk change. Focus on creating a streamlined, customer-driven team that can respond quickly and flexibly to the amazing changes taking place in the world around us.

> "How will we solve crime, poverty, homelessness? By acting collectively. How do we act collectively? Through government."
>
> — David Osborne
> & Ted Gaebler,
> Reinventing Government

WHAT WILL PEOPLE SAY?

The Killer Phrase that gives your organization permission to keep up with the Joneses. Or stay behind with them. But never ever get ahead.

> a/k/a: *The union will scream.*
> *Top management will never go for it.*
> *You can't do that here.*
> *Let's stay in step.*

Shift the naysayer's perspective from concern to collaboration with one of these strategies.

Right question, wrong vision. The naysayer predicts an immediate, negative reaction to a revolutionary new idea. Extend the focus even further into the future. What will the "people" say, see, hear, and feel...when the problem is *solved*?

Be a "people" person. Step into other people's shoes by talking with everyone who has a stake in your idea. Identify people who have supported new ideas in the past and enlist them as your cheerleaders and champions.

> "Where you stand on an issue depends on where you sit."
>
> — *Murphy's Law*

LEADERSHIP ACTION

To solve tough problems, help your people visualize a successful future where cooperation exists and the problem is solved. Then, work backwards to the present to identify intermediate actions.

Consider new alliances that unite traditional opponents. In organizations such as Saturn, Xerox and Goodyear, union workers and management leaders are learning to focus their energies on creating a quality product together.

COMPARATIVE THINKING

"Wellington is a bad general; the English are bad soldiers. We will settle this matter by lunchtime." — *Napoleon I of France, at Waterloo, 1815*

"As to Bell's talking telegraph, it only creates interest in scientific circles... its commercial values will be limited." — *Elisha Gray, inventor, 1876*

"Heavier-than-air flying machines are impossible."
— *Lord Kelvin, Royal Society president, 1895*

"No mere machine will replace a reliable and honest clerk."
— *president of Remington Arms Company rejecting patent rights for the typewriter, 1897*

"Television won't be able to hold on to any market it captures after the first six months. People will soon get tired of staring at a plywood box every night."
— *Daryl F. Zanuck, head of 20th Century Fox, 1946*

> * **Benchmarking: the continuous process of measuring products, services and practices against the toughest competitors and recognized leaders.**
>
> — *Xerox Corporation*

My dog's bigger than your dog. Our firm won the contract. He's younger. She's prettier. We all use benchmarking* to place ourselves in context within the world. That's fine...to a point.

Shakespeare may have been talking about Killer Phrases when he remarked that comparisons are odious. The Killer Phrases in this section represent benchmarking's evil twin. They compare apples to oranges, fact to fiction, new challenges to glorified history. All with a single goal: to justify keeping innovation at a safe distance.

You can help Comparative Thinkers reframe their reality to ensure a fair comparison – and a fair chance for your idea.

WE'VE ALWAYS DONE IT THIS WAY.

Ye Olde Killer Phrase. Tradition is admirable, but smart organizations know that complacency can lead to collapse.

> *a/k/a: Let's stick with what works.*
> *It's change for the sake of change.*
> *We've done alright so far.*

Break this endless loop with one or more of the following strategies.

Put "it" in perspective. Think together for a moment. Is there anything in life that hasn't evolved? Recall examples by saying, "At one time we believed that [...] would never work and it has been a surprising success."

Don't argue apples and oranges. Agree that the old way was good for its time. Show how things have changed, and how new ideas lead to new successes. Support your idea with concrete examples such as fixed-price cars, invoiceless billing and crystal-clear colas. New times demand new thinking.

Identify the core rule. What stated or implied belief does the existing method support? Is that still valid? Maybe it's time for Spring Cleaning.

LEADERSHIP ACTION

Remember the questions you asked as a new hire:

> *Why do we have to fill out that form?*
> *Who's in charge of this?*
> *What if...?*

Most of these questions occur during a person's first three months in a new job or job task. After that, employees adopt company policy and stop asking. Keep the questions alive by spending 10% of each staff meeting challenging a different ingrained assumption.

> "Experts are those who don't bother with dumb questions anymore — thus they fail to see the bottlenecks buried in 'We've always done it that way!'"
>
> — *Tom Peters,*
> Thriving on Chaos

BI

IT'S TOO FAR AHEAD OF ITS TIME.

BUT

An idea is a thought not yet anchored to a time frame. Everything you see around you was once a stretch of the imagination. From flashlights to fax machines, most great ideas have been ahead of their time. Thank goodness. Who wants a new idea that is behind its time? Or even on time? By the time you had said it out loud, its time would be up.

> a/k/a: *It has never been tried before.*
> *It's too radical for us.*
> *Can we get back to reality?*

Your idea has highlighted a problem, a gap between present state (business as usual) and future state (successful implementation of your idea). The naysayer is having difficulty crossing that gap. Find out the reason for not crossing, state a benefit, and build a bridge.

It's too much, too fast. The gap is too big to bridge with one jump. Shift the focus from light years ahead to just 15 minutes ahead by showing your idea's immediate benefits. Consider building a prototype or conducting a field test.

I can't see it. Put your vision-driven solution in present terms by explaining desired outcomes as specific, positive results. What will people see, hear, and feel when your idea is reality?

We can't afford to make mistakes. Explore future consequences of not implementing the idea. Conduct a little time travel. If the group continues business as usual, what will the business look like in five years?

LEADERSHIP ACTION

To encourage great ideas, think like Walt Disney: "If you can dream it... you can do it." As a leader, you want ideas that are light years ahead. You need to see far enough down the road to guide your company.

The best idea is 15 minutes ahead of its time. Those that are light years ahead get ignored.

— *paraphrasing Woody Allen, filmmaker*

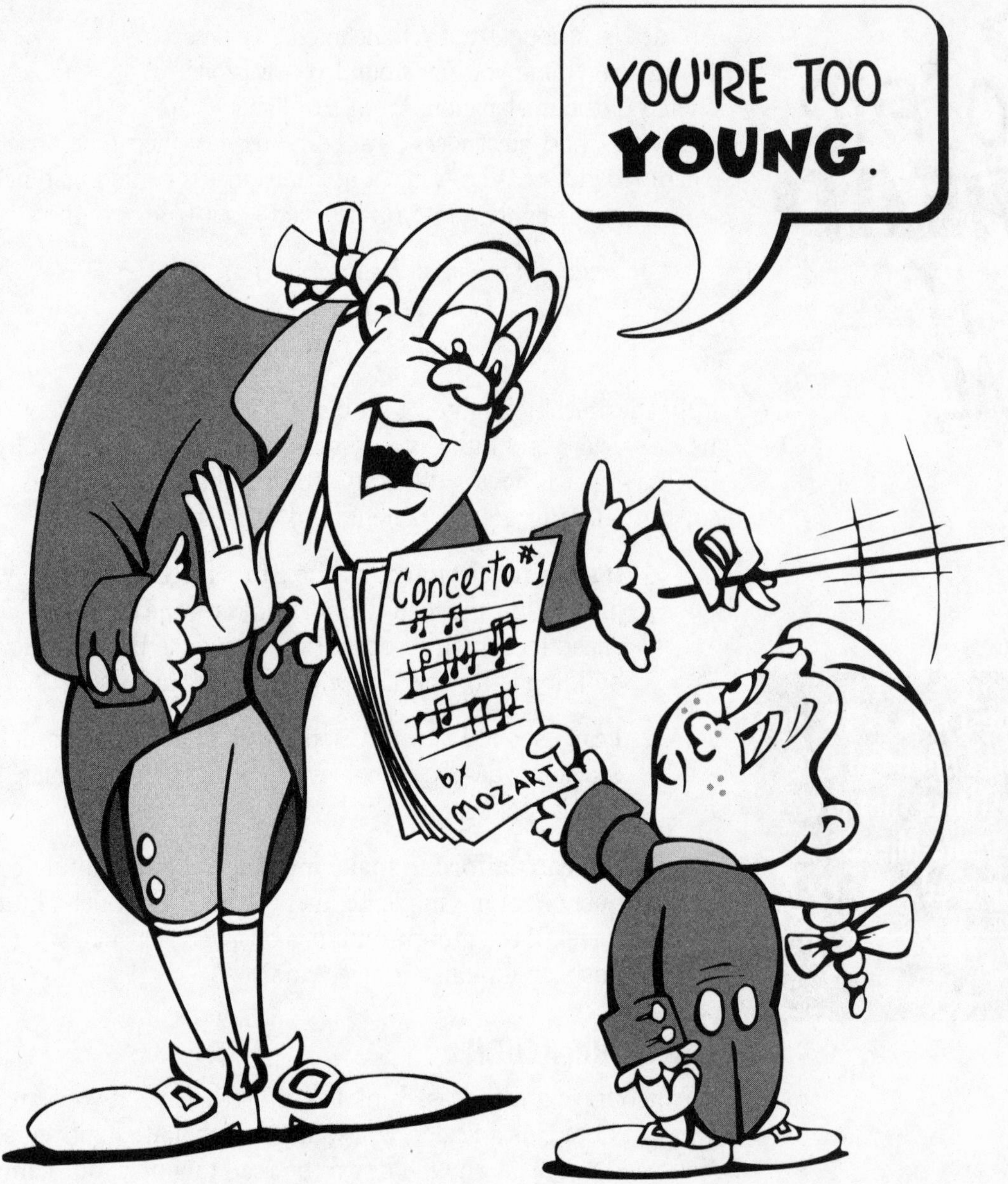
YOU'RE TOO YOUNG.
Concerto #1
by MOZART

YOU'RE TOO YOUNG.

This Catch-22 of Killer Phrases can attack from outside or within us. We're at our most creative when we are young, but credibility takes time.

> *a/k/a:*   *You don't have the training.*
> *Who let Junior in here?*
> *Get a little experience under your belt first.*

Separate content issues from personnel issues to diffuse this parental Killer Phrase before you're over the hill!

Act your age. The young perspective is fresh, uncluttered by preconceived notions. Establish your unique view as a bridge, rather than a barrier to the solution.

Do your homework. The younger you are and the bigger your idea is, the wider the leap of faith will be between the naysayer's current reality and your vision. Move beyond initial blocks to constructive reasoning by grounding your idea in relevant research and documentation.

Share. Established professionals may feel threatened if the new kid is on the verge of solving a problem that has baffled them for years. Invite collaboration so colleagues can share the recognition.

Speak the language. Don't let a generation gap become a language barrier. Present your idea in terms that your audience can understand and appreciate.

LEADERSHIP ACTION

Kids.... What will they think of next? You'd better listen. This Killer Phrase often sends young employees away from a parent company to start their own. Build a strong, committed organization by recognizing the values, interests, and needs of all employees.

> **Four-year-old Mozart composed a concerto "so extraordinarily difficult no one would be able to play it."**
>
> — *Johann Schachtner, court trumpeter*

YOU'RE OVER THE HILL.

BUT

COMPARATIVE THINKING

Just when you thought your idea had made it safely past "You're too young"...surprise! Naysayers never rest.

a/k/a: *Never trust anyone over thirty/forty/fifty.*
Let the young people worry about that.
Sit back and relax – you've earned it.
Shouldn't you be thinking about your retirement?

Try one of these strategies to help your new-born idea reach maturity.

Be a mentor. Draw from your marvelous perspective to become the catalyst for innovation and the management champion to expedite new ideas through channels.

Place it in context. Use concrete examples and the right language to show that your idea is timely or ahead of its time – anything but behind the times!

LEADERSHIP ACTION

Call upon mature staff as a resource to build each team with at least one "bureaucracy buster."

Avoid the age-old stereotype that equates older with old hat. Ben Franklin discovered electricity after he retired. Colonel Harland Sanders launched his fried chicken empire at sixty-five years *young*.

I HAVE A BETTER IDEA.

Creative hitchhike or Killer Phrase? Hitchhiking on ideas is a great brainstorming technique. Unfortunately, "I have a better idea" often signals a game of one-upmanship. The stakes: power and turf.

a/k/a: *There are better ways than that.*
        That gives me a better idea.

Reframe or bypass the power play with one of these approaches.

Swiped with pride. Be pleased that your recommendation was a hitchhike to a supposedly better solution. Ideas are free associations and can always be improved.

Second team. Help make the "better" idea successful by offering your idea as a back-up, if the first idea stumbles.

Teaming up. Explore the qualities of both ideas to offset weaknesses from one with strengths from the other.

> "A great leader is one whose followers say, 'We did it ourselves.'"
>
> — *Lao-tzu,*
> *legendary Chinese sage*

LEADERSHIP ACTION

People no longer expect leaders to have every right answer. They do, however, expect leaders to provide a playing field for trying out new ideas. When you put new ideas into play, encourage others to improve on them.

OVERGENERALIZATION ———— BUT

"Everything that can be invented has been invented."
— *Charles Duell, U.S. Patent Office director, 1899*

"There is no likelihood man can ever tap the power of the atom."
— *Robert Millikan, Nobel Prize–winning physicist, 1923*

"It is impossible to sell animal stories in the U.S.A."
— *publisher, rejecting George Orwell's* Animal Farm, *1945*

"Groups with guitars are on their way out."
— *Decca Records, turning down the Beatles, 1962*

"There is no reason for any individual to have a computer in his home."
— *Ken Olsen, president of Digital Equipment, 1977*

Yes/no. Good/bad. Always/never. Overgeneralizers are binary. Overgeneralizers save time. Overgeneralizers have already decided key issues BEFORE they hear your idea. Extreme? Possibly. Efficient? Probably. Idea-deadly? Definitely.

True, educated opinions are based on a collection of past experiences. But most of the ideas and inventions we take for granted wouldn't exist if Overgeneralizers throughout history had had their way.

The chink in the always/never armor is the Exception to the Rule. Turn "never" into "ever," "can't" into "can" – and your idea into reality.

> **"...divergent problems offend the logical mind, which wishes to remove tension by coming down on one side or the other."**
> — *E.F. Schumacher,*
> A Guide for the Perplexed

IT'LL NEVER WORK!

A door-slamming, ego-deflating idea squasher suitable for business, home-repair projects or play.

> *a/k/a:* *It'll never fly.*
> *It'll never sell.*
> *It'll never win approval.*

Open doors and minds to a new way of doing things.

Create a working definition. Often the core issue is different definitions of the verb "to work." Here's a quick quiz.

Does "to work" mean:
- ❏ 100% perfection?
- ❏ zero defects?
- ❏ leaping tall buildings in a single bound?
- ❏ producing a desired result?

Does the naysayer's definition match yours? If not, establish criteria for success. Ask how well the initial idea has to work to be beneficial.

Change the rules. From bumblebee flight to quantum physics, some of life's greatest achievements shouldn't work. Often, the only thing not working is our old way of viewing the problem. Use new images, new words and "What if...?" questions to inspire a little upside-down thinking and give your idea some "working" room.

LEADERSHIP ACTION

Replace "It'll never work" in your own conversations with:

> *Can we do a test first to see the results?*
> *Where do you think this will work best?*
> *What will it take to make this work?*

Encourage commitment to working it out!

> "It's always fun to do the impossible."
>
> — *Walt Disney,*
> *animation pioneer*

WHOSO PULLETH THE SWORD FROM THE STONE IS
RIGHTWISE KING OF ENGLAND . . .

WE TRIED THAT BEFORE.

The naysayer's adage: "If at first you don't succeed...drop it!"

> *a/k/a:* *That's been done to death.*
> *They've been coming up with that one for years.*
> *I've heard that one a million times.*
> *Not that again.*

Diagram this sentence to uncover the root cause.

"We." Who was "we"? Were they empowered to succeed? Did they have adequate resources? At one time, some people in the organization believed in this idea. Rekindle that support and show that, with backing, additional knowledge, and new circumstances, the idea can succeed this time.

"Tried." How hard did they try? For how long? Compare current and past situations to show that it is time for another try.

"That." True, something about your idea sounds familiar – but probably not identical. Find similarities and differences. Highlight the new twists in your idea. Take advantage of past learning to strengthen your approach.

"Before." When? Under what circumstances? Demonstrate that conditions have changed, offering an entirely new arena for the idea. Listen for conditions that haven't changed and may hinder your idea's success. Look for ways to change or adapt to them.

LEADERSHIP ACTION

Be careful, especially with new employees, not to greet every new idea with "We've tried that before" – even if you have. Try adding open-ended questions, such as "What did we learn from before?" and "How have circumstances changed?"

> **"Dixie Cups, Life Savers...were conceived, failed and reborn"** thanks to ingenuity, enthusiasm and determination.
>
> — *Michael Gershman,*
> *Getting It Right the*
> *Second Time*

IT'LL BE MORE **TROUBLE** THAN IT'S WORTH.

Feel a new idea coming on? This Killer Phrase invites you to just lie down until the feeling goes away.

> *a/k/a:*   *We'd lose in the long run.*
> *Why bother?*
> *It won't pay for itself.*
> *It'll cause more problems than it solves.*
> *That's hopelessly complex.*

Go from troublesome to trouble-free with one or more of these strategies.

Trouble or opportunity? Anticipate best potential opportunities and worst possible troubles to make an informed decision.

Why stir up trouble? To command attention and resources, most ideas must meet a bottom-line need. Put yourself in the naysayer's shoes and visualize "What's in It for Me?" to adopt your solution. Create a win-win partnership with immediate and long-term benefits.

Return on Investment. Weigh resource costs against potential gains. How much gain is required to justify piloting your idea? If your idea takes more effort to explain, approve or implement than it saves, you may need to refine your original concept. Or shift your solution to another problem.

LEADERSHIP ACTION

You snooze, you lose. Create an organization that looks for trouble – and does something about it! Take advantage of the opportunity gap between problem and solution as a source of creative energy.

> "The things we fear most in organizations – fluctuations, disturbances, imbalances – ...are the primary source of creativity."
>
> — *Margaret J. Wheatley,*
> Leadership and the New Science

YOU CAN'T TEACH AN OLD DOG NEW TRICKS.

> **Our moms are two late-blooming computer whiz kids. One has a desktop Mac, the other a laptop clone.**
>
> — *the authors*

Actually, you probably can. Has anyone asked the dog?

> *a/k/a:* *Our customers aren't that sophisticated.*
> *It would never work in government.*
> *We've got to wait for the old generation to retire.*

Don't roll over and play dead – speak! Sniff out the issues.

The Dog. Show that the naysayer is barking up the wrong tree. The statement may be true, but only under certain conditions. Long-time employees may simply not understand what they must do to keep pace with the organization.

The Trick. The word "trick" implies a fake, a quick fix. Is this the tenth new trick these old dogs have been asked to perform? Did anyone care when they accomplished the first nine? Learn past history so that you can show why your idea is much more than the latest trick.

The Naysayer. Maybe this person doesn't want change. Typical reasons to avoid change include perceived loss of power, esteem, and security. Find the reason for the resistance and neutralize it.

LEADERSHIP ACTION

Encourage ongoing learning in and around your organization. Tell old clients about new ideas. Tell success stories about older employees who have broken the mold. Use the changes sweeping our planet as a metaphor for our continuing ability to grow.

35

PEOPLE DON'T WANT CHANGE.

Look around you. Ironic, isn't it? This naysayer's license to stop growing is probably the only thing that has not changed.

> a/k/a: *People are creatures of habit – they'll never buy it.*
> *It sounds too complicated.*
> *That's not consistent with the way we do things here.*
> *You'll offend 90% of our audience.*

Move from impossible to empowered with one of these strategies.

Create opportunities for buy-in. Determine who will be affected by your recommendation. Then, build time and dialogue into the change process so that everyone involved can develop a personal stake in the idea's success.

Demonstrate change. We often view the status quo as a safe island that we are reluctant to leave. According to John Sculley, long-time CEO of Apple, we're so busy wanting things NOT to happen that we tend to look at the world through a "rearview mirror." Provide current examples to show that, in reality, we are in the midst of constant internal and external change.

Identify rewards. What will make your suggestion worthwhile? Typical reasons include enhanced job status and financial security. The desire for freedom has people demanding change – witness the wave of democracy sweeping our planet.

LEADERSHIP ACTION

Encourage creative destruction by helping people escape from old ideas to make room for new ones. How? Pull out an old business plan and show it to your staff. What was considered fact just a few years ago now probably seems more like fiction. Demonstrate that change was unexpected and, in most cases, beneficial.

> **You can never cross the same river because the water is always changing.**
>
> — *Ancient philosophy*

PUT-DOWNS

"What use could the company make of an electric toy?"
— *Western Union, rejecting rights to Alexander Graham Bell's telephone, 1878*

"What? You would make a ship sail against the wind by lighting a bonfire under her decks? I have no time to listen to such nonsense!"
— *Napoleon I of France, discussing Robert Fulton's steam engine*

"I'm sorry, Mr. Kipling, but you just don't know how to use the English language."
— *publisher, rejecting Rudyard Kipling, 1889*

"...the automobile is only a novelty – a fad."
— *Michigan Savings Bank president advising a colleague against investing in Ford Motor Company*

Zing! Pow! Fwap. Smash. Meet the Put-downs, those pseudo-powerful Killer Phrases designed to keep your new idea "in its place."

Yes, efficiency and stability often depend on some type of pecking order. But Put-downs are the trademark, automatic response of any dysfunctional hierarchy. From executives to managers to staff. From parents to teenagers to children. Culturally defined Put-downs run rampant down the ranks of unhealthy organizations, those branded "learning disabled" by MIT's Peter Senge. Look behind the manager who utters a Put-down and you'll likely find an executive who said it first.

Like other addictive behaviors, Put-downs benefit from intervention. This section can help you stop putting up with put-downs.

> **"Instead of supervising and giving feedback, many of us 'parent' our employees ...demanding respect and compliance 'because we said so.'"**
>
> — *Amy Stark, Ph.D.,*
> Because I Said So

Nyet. Não. Non. Nein. Ner. Throughout history and around the globe, this one word can bring conversation and innovation to a full stop.

> *a/k/a:* No way.
> NOT!
> I don't think so.
> That doesn't have a snowball's chance in hell.

Use your know-how to move from "NO!" to "Let's go!"

Remember, You ≠ Your Idea. Before taking this Killer Phrase personally, find out if the naysayer is simply buying time or having a bad day.

Don't create a win-lose situation. Be consultative rather than combative. Ask questions and explain why you're asking. Allow adversarial opinions to coexist with yours to create a stronger solution.

Make it easy to say "yes." Or even "maybe." Begin with simple points of agreement to get naysayers saying "yes" immediately. Identify reasons for resistance and offer to handle them personally.

Check your negatives. Before your presentation, spend time thinking of all the reasons someone else would say "no" to your idea. Are you willing to counter their arguments?

> "Nothing, not all the armies in the world, can stop an idea whose time has come."
>
> — *Victor Hugo, writer*

LEADERSHIP ACTION

"No" is the first thing many of us remember our parents saying. Is it the first thing employees remember you saying? Do a self-check. How many times per day do you say "no"? (Parents average 432!) Is your "no" really "no," or just a test to see how committed the idea proposers are? Be specific about what it would take to turn your "no" into "yes," such as investing their own time into the project.

THE WORLD'S FIRST KILLER PHRASE

BECAUSE I *SAID* SO.

This last-ditch response by parents to children's endless "why's," becomes the naysayer's immunization against new ideas.

> a/k/a: Didn't you read my memo?!
> It turns me off.
> I don't like it.
> I've already told you...

Go from solid resistance to steadfast support with one of these strategies.

Who's saying it? This may be a responsibility issue. Offer to accept full responsibility for the idea. Ask if the naysayer is willing to accept full responsibility for not pursuing the idea. Determine whether someone with different responsibilities would view your idea differently. Is that person higher up the ladder?

Why? Determine whether the naysayer is speaking out of frustration or a lack of time. Perhaps the organization had a bad experience with a similar idea.

> **Ask why your problem is occurring. Then counter your answer with "Why?" four more times.**
>
> — *Toyota Motors*

LEADERSHIP ACTION

Be a role model. Check your own conscience for any sacred cows that need to be put to pasture. On which subjects can people validate your opinions but not question them? Outlaw "because I said so" to show that your organization is confident enough to act on *all* the facts.

Take a tip from organizations such as Sprint who aggressively seek the underlying cause of knotty problems. Encourage your people to ask "why."

HA! HA! HA!

> "If an idea does not appear bizarre, there is no hope for it."
>
> — *Niels Bohr, physicist*

A favorite creativity axiom is, "If everyone says you're wrong, you're one step ahead. If everyone laughs at you, you're two steps ahead." Accept the laughter and run with it. You have a head start.

> *a/k/a:*   ...fake smile...
>   ...rolled eyes...
>   *You've got to be joking.*

Make laughter the best medicine for your new idea with one of these healthy prescriptions.

In good company. Recall other laughable ideas that are now success stories. Perhaps you've heard about the baby bottle nipple company that decided to make condoms. At first everyone laughed and said condoms would be self-defeating to the industry. Now the company is positioned for profit in any market and laughing all the way to the bank. So, agree that your idea is way out there, then ground it with a benefit statement.

Times change. In the '50s, the U.S. laughed at Japan's quality. In the '90s, we have Sony, Nintendo, Lexus, extended warranties.... Who's laughing now?

Smile back. Sound simple? Yes, and effective. Returning a smile builds rapport, sets a tone of equality and encourages conversation. It makes you feel better, too.

LEADERSHIP ACTION

Encourage healthy laughter as a bridge to creativity and discovery. Scientist-author Lewis Thomas uses laughter as a barometer: "Whenever you can hear laughter...something probably worth looking at has begun to happen in the lab."

STONE AGE BRAINSTORMING

IDEAS ARE A DIME A DOZEN.

This old favorite has survived inflation, taxation, depression, and recession. But the cost of ignoring new ideas is too high a price to pay in any economy.

> a/k/a: *So what else is new?*
> *Your idea and a dollar will buy a cup of coffee.*
> *It's not your money we're spending.*
> *Not ANOTHER idea!*
> *Talk is cheap.*
> *Is that it?*

Shift the focus from pocket change to promoting change with one of these change-making strategies.

Cheaper by the dozen. The best way to get great ideas is to get lots of ideas and throw the bad ones away. Invite the naysayer to "free" associate with you to come up with a dozen ideas, then offer to be the person who weeds them out.

Up the ante. Suggest that the two of you spend a dollar on two cups of coffee and discuss your idea.

Agree. Interpret this Killer Phrase as a cry for action. The money comes from implementing the idea. Show how your idea can turn a dime into a diamond mine.

LEADERSHIP ACTION

Call for "turn-on-a-dime" action. Pick one idea and explore the possibilities. Steven Spielberg claims that if you don't act on your ideas, they will pop out of your head and into someone else's. Probably your competitor's.

Union Carbide employees' ideas generated an additional $20 million in reengineering savings — "50% more than management expected."

— *Thomas A. Stewart,*
"Reengineering," Fortune

THE BIRTH OF WRITER'S BLOCK

DON'T BE RIDICULOUS.

A quite profound, albeit short-sighted Killer Phrase. Photocopiers. Overnight delivery. Round-the-clock news. Car phones with voice mail. I mean, really. Don't be ridiculous.

> a/k/a: *Are you crazy?*
> *Sure...and I'm an astronaut.*
> *Be practical.*
> *NEXT!*

Is the core issue your idea, or the frivolous tone it brings to the environment? Let one person break through sterile, starchy business as usual, and we risk total anarchy by lunchtime.

> **Look at your idea.** How can you win acceptance without ridicule? Make your concepts credible by using metaphors, showing benefits, and relating to similar successful ideas. Make your concepts easy to understand by simplifying the language and breaking your idea into small chunks.

> **Look at the context.** Put your idea on a continuum and examine the extremes. If this is the most ridiculous, what's the most logical? Can you move your idea closer to "logical" by adding statistics, reports, endorsements or exhibits?

LEADERSHIP ACTION

To paraphrase Aristotle, "When you need a smart answer, ask a dumb question."

> *What if we shipped all overnight express packages to a central distribution hub?*
> *What if we moved computing power to the employees' desktops?*
> *What if we televised news 24 hours a day, 7 days a week?*

Ask a ridiculous question today.

> "The man with a new idea is a crank until he succeeds."
>
> — *Mark Twain, humorist*

YOU AND WHOSE ARMY WILL CARRY IT OFF?

Be all that you can be – as long as it doesn't require resources.

> *a/k/a:* *Our computer can't handle it.*
> *There are land mines out there.*

Draft support for your idea with one of these strategies.

Put first things first. Evaluate the idea before you worry about mobilizing the forces. Consider a field trial that tests your idea and vividly demonstrates proposed benefits to your organization.

A few good wo/men. Think small. Show how you can achieve the same goal with a squad, rather than a company-sized battalion.

Employ guerrilla tactics. Think like a renegade – what can you adapt from other resources to support your new idea? Is the naysayer willing to put in any resources at all, or are you totally on your own?

LEADERSHIP ACTION

Focusing on full-scale deployment in today's workplace may mean that your troops are left...left...left behind. Do you need an army or will a SWAT team get the job done?

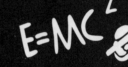
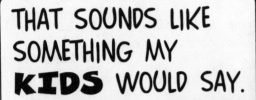

THAT SOUNDS LIKE SOMETHING MY **KIDS** WOULD SAY.

Adolescent idea breaking out? Not to worry. This Clearasil of Killer Phrases dries it up faster than you can say Bart Simpson.

> *a/k/a:*   *Are you kidding?*
> *Have you given it much thought?*
> *People will say we're silly.*
> *That's really off the wall.*
> *Come on now, get serious.*
> *My seven-year-old could do better than that.*

Move beyond childish constraints without losing the childlike charm.

Out of the mouths of babes.... Dumb questions often reveal smart answers. Show that your group may be too close to this "adult" problem.

It's grown-up time. Does the naysayer believe you haven't thought the issues through? People sometimes equate youth with lack of preparation or thought. Ground recommendations by considering strengths and weaknesses and backing up your claims with concrete evidence.

It's playtime. Agree with the Killer Phrase. Then, suggest that the two of you just "play" with the idea for a minute, before you evaluate it.

> "Man is most nearly himself when he approaches the serious-ness of a child at play."
>
> — Heraclitus, *philosopher*

LEADERSHIP ACTION

All kidding aside, kids' views are becoming powerful views. Children seek out experiences adults often avoid, spending big money in the process. The child's fresh perspective now drives many initiatives in the public and private sectors, including specially targeted presidential press conferences, news shows, travel services, food, fashion, and music. Take time to discover the views of your children and those of your "inner child."

WHY DON'T YOU GO HOME EARLY TODAY?

This semi-serious Killer Phrase says there's no place like home to dampen those little gray cells of innovation. But the joke's on the naysayer with this one. With worldwide connectivity from the desktop and round-the-clock services, "Why don't you go home" could be the ultimate invitation to creativity in the '90s.

> *a/k/a:*   *Perhaps it's time for that vacation.*
> *Have you been feeling alright?*
> *Just leave it with me. I'll work on it.*
> *Let's sleep on it.*

Show that continuous improvement is where your heart is, with one of these home-spun approaches.

Say "thanks!" State that you'd like to work on this idea more at home. Further sell your project by demonstrating your willingness to invest your own time as needed.

Clear the decks. Has the suggestion made the naysayer uncomfortable? Maybe the organization can't handle it – it's too big a creative stretch or considered to be unsafe. Gauge the reaction: does being sent home equate to a fire drill or a bomb scare?

Go outside and play. Suggest a walk together around the block to break out of the usual thinking "box" and discuss the idea.

LEADERSHIP ACTION

Did you know that most great ideas come when we're away from work? Find out where and when your people come up with their best ideas. Adapt work habits to honor these idea-friendly environments. Changes may be as simple as a mid-afternoon walk, or as fundamental as telecommuting and flex-time.

Top 10 Idea-Friendly Times:

10. Cutting the grass
9. Listening to a dull sermon
8. Waking up during the night
7. Exercising
6. Reading for pleasure
5. Sitting in a boring meeting
4. Falling asleep or waking up
3. Commuting to work
2. Showering or shaving
1. Sitting on the toilet!

— *from* What a Great Idea!

IT ISN'T *YOUR* RESPONSIBILITY.

The Killer Phrase postcard that says outside-the-box thinking is a nice place to visit, but you can't possibly live there.

> *a/k/a:*   *That's not your department.*
> *You're overextended.*
> *Let the other guys take the risk.*
> *That isn't in your job description.*
> *Not your problem.*

Reframe the situation to show why your involvement is a key to success.

Present a new view. Those in positions of responsibility are often too close to the problem. When managers at IBM Credit shifted their perspective from internal specialist to external sales representative, they immediately discovered ways to reduce overhead, increase productivity – and trim a six-day application process to four hours.

Empower yourself. Is the naysayer afraid you'll get too involved in the new idea and then get behind in your work? If you're committed to testing your idea, offer to work on it after-hours.

Share the vision. In today's workplace, organizational success is everyone's responsibility. Show how the problem is affecting your organization's core beliefs.

Become a catalyst. Explain how you can champion innovation by helping to speed up processes...to knock down bureaucracy... to cut through red tape....

> "The significant problems in life cannot be solved from the same mode that created them."
>
> — *Albert Einstein, physicist*

LEADERSHIP ACTION

Take your organization to the leading edge by evaluating ideas based on merit, not job function. GE, Dep Corporation, and Steelcase, Inc., break hierarchical stereotypes to invite shared visions and boundaryless thinking. The next time you need an innovative solution try asking, "What would happen if we viewed this problem from a different perspective?"

DON'T WASTE YOUR TIME THINKING.

The Killer Phrase equivalent of a pat on the head. "There, there...," the naysayer coos, "let the grown-ups handle this one." Or, equally damaging, the naysayer sympathizes but believes the situation is so out of your control that you might as well give up before you begin. (The naysayer might even be you.)

> *a/k/a:*   *Don't worry your pretty little head about that.*
> *I'm the one who gets paid to think around here.*
> *You've got enough to think about.*
> *If you're so smart, why aren't you rich?*
> *What makes you think you are smarter than the experts?*

Is it really a time issue?

If YES: What constitutes a "waste of time"? How much time? Whose? It may be time to take time – to reengineer* processes rather than simply revise procedures.

If NO: It's probably one of the Rules of Bureaucracy, such as: The boss is always right. Counter it with a dose of empowerment.

LEADERSHIP ACTION

Continuous improvement requires input from all levels, with several "right" answers. The next time you have to make a decision that affects your staff, call a time-out on the formal hierarchy. Gather ideas from everyone to create a team solution. Empowered teams often set – and achieve – the toughest standards.

Limit thinking to the experts, and you could be limiting your organization's potential and focus. Datsun experts named their new car the "Fair Lady," based on U.S. market research; someone "not paid to think" renamed it the 240 Z.

* **Reengineering:** "fundamental rethinking and radical redesign of business processes to achieve dramatic improvements in performance ...doing more with less."

— *Michael Hammer & James Champy,* Reengineering the Corporation

THE BOSS WILL NEVER GO FOR IT.

This show-stopping Killer Phrase gives your idea the thumbs down before the curtain even rises.

> a/k/a: What will they say upstairs?
> The boss will eat you alive.
> There's a reason this organization isn't a democracy.

Shift the perspective to turn a poor dress rehearsal into a great performance.

You're the boss. Step into the chief's shoes for a moment and brainstorm why the boss would never go for it. Now, step back into your own. Which reasons give you additional information to strengthen your idea? How many negative reasons can you turn around?

Go to the opposite. Restate the Killer Phrase as a question: "When would the boss go for it?" Ask yourself whether your competitor's boss would go for it and why.

LEADERSHIP ACTION

As a boss or manager, are you a stepping stone to innovation – or a stumbling block to progress? Your expertise may create a filter that only the blandest of new ideas can survive. Encourage divergent thinking throughout your organization by engaging in it yourself and by showing that you don't have all the right answers.

> "Freedom is good, but control is better."
>
> — Nikolai Lenin,
> Russian Communist leader

SELECTIVE EDITING

"There's no use trying. One can't believe impossible things."
— *Alice in Lewis Carroll's* Through the Looking Glass, *1872*

"Sensible and responsible women do not want the right to vote."
— *Grover Cleveland, president of the United States, 1905*

"The world capacity for computers is five." — *Thomas Watson, Sr., founder of IBM, 1943*

"We don't know who first discovered water, but we can be sure it wasn't a fish."
— *Marshall McLuhan, academician*

"We enter school as question marks and graduate as periods."
— *John Holt, educational critic*

"Age 7 – Why? Age 17 – Why not? Age 37 – Because." — *David Campbell, author*

Each of us takes in new information through a unique set of filters. At its worst, this filtering process causes us to hear only what we wish to hear, see only what we wish to see. Selective Editors wear Killer Phrase-colored glasses, causing them to see each new idea from the same, short-sighted viewpoint. But from women in politics to computers in virtually every business and home, we are surrounded by proof that people can and do change their perspective.

Established organizations are moving beyond traditional filters to rediscover success. "Business as usual" in the '90s means boundaryless environments and the death of parochialism.*

This section helps you expand tunnel vision, cross functional barriers, and break through "not invented here" mindsets to give your ideas the filter change they deserve.

> *** Parochialism: a corporate syndrome characterized by narrow views, limited range and "if we did not invent it here, it can't possibly be any good."**
>
> — GE Annual Report

SAYS WHO?!

The safe sex of Killer Phrases. This cautious naysayer will not engage in dialogue until you state exactly where your idea has been.

> *a/k/a:* *What will they say in [...]?*
> *We don't have the authority.*
> *What would the [...] say?*
> *Did you get approval for this?*

Move from detrimental delegation to empowered action with one of these strategies.

Say what? Did you catch the naysayer off guard or strike a nerve? Help the person recover and put the new idea into perspective by narrowing its focus and grounding it with concrete examples.

Answer the real questions. Who are your supporters? How qualified and powerful are they? What evidence do you have that people who support your idea will look good?

Know Who's Who. Before you formally present your idea, interview the people who will be affected by it. Cultivate some grass-roots support. Identify potential risks and quantify benefits.

> The microwave oven was invented by an "inquisitive, self-educated...engineer who never finished grammar school."
>
> — *Ira Flatow,*
> They All Laughed

LEADERSHIP ACTION

Do your employees buy into empowerment? Do you? The willingness to delegate authority is a common struggle as organizations flatten out. Determine whether your people have bought into the new values, or are just going through the motions.

GE CEO Jack Welch's 1992 message to stockholders was clear: Managers who meet task commitments but don't believe in empowerment, participative management, and collaborative support are out. Personal success is not enough – true leaders also make others successful.

WE HAVEN'T GOT THE PERSONNEL.

How many people does it take to launch a new idea? With this Killer Phrase it only takes one naysayer to sink it.

> a/k/a: *We're too busy to do that.*
> *There are only so many hours in a day.*
> *We're cutting people, not adding them.*

Do a little crowd control on this blanket statement with one of these ideas.

Work within the system. Determine what kind of test you can do with existing personnel. Sell your idea to other departments to tap additional resources. Bring in contract or part-time workers to test the idea.

Do more with less. State clearly the productivity increase your idea will bring. Show how the new idea optimizes resources – time, money, people – so you can either bring in more people or you don't need as many.

Turn it around. Would you *lose* key personnel if you didn't implement this idea? Would you outdate yourselves or lose market share? Show that your group can't afford NOT to act on your suggestion.

LEADERSHIP ACTION

Look past existing personnel levels to create a work team for the life of the test. Companies like MCI are making temporary and contract employees the fastest growing job sector – estimated near 40% by the year 2000.

> "The hottest new kind of company: no employees...outsource everything...the virtual corporation."
>
> — *"Virtual Realities,"* Inc. *magazine*

GREAT IDEA, **BUT** NOT FOR US.

Beware tunnel vision. The light at the end of the tunnel may be an oncoming train.

> a/k/a: This place is different.
> That's not our problem.
> It might work in your department, but not in mine.
> Are you working for the competition?
> We're not ready for that yet.

Broaden the focus with one of these strategies.

20/20 Hindsight. Help the naysayer visit the future where your idea has succeeded. Then, look back.

Put first things first. Would it be a great idea for the team after solving some other problems? If so, focus on the bigger problems to clear the way for your great idea.

Dissect it. Is there a part of the idea that is for your organization?

Translate it. A language gap may create additional barriers to your idea. Describe your suggestion in terms that allow you and the naysayer to work from the same vision.

Look around. Don't get discouraged. A failed proposal simply means you've found the solution to a different problem! Save your ideas in an Idea Bank.*

LEADERSHIP ACTION

Create environments that reach across traditional boundaries. Steelcase, Inc., has offices set up as clusters of desks with no two people from the same department sitting next to each other. This "cross-functional" approach builds a dialogue that enhances solutions and sparks innovation.

Ask "How would our competitors solve this?" and learn from the answers.

---

* **Idea Bank: the place you record ideas so that they are available, retrievable...visible.**

- Computer database
- Card file
- Notebook
- Refrigerator door

Saved ideas are like money in the bank.

— *from* What a Great Idea!

IT'S NOT IN THE BUDGET.

Coming to market six months late but on budget earns 33% less profit over five years. Coming out on time and 50% over budget cuts profits only 4%.

— *McKinsey and Company*

A favorite response, especially by accountants, this Killer Phrase puts formal, bureaucratic muscle behind anything to do with dollars and cents – or dollars and sense.

a/k/a: *Don't you know there's a recession going on?*
There's no such thing as a free lunch.
Do you think money grows on trees?
Just wait 'til they run the numbers.

Move beyond funding issues to fundamental changes with one of these bottom-line approaches.

Think like an entrepreneur. If this were your company, how would you fund your great idea? Would you spend [...]% of your own money to try this idea?

Know thy budget. Be prepared to sell your idea and separate realistic budgetary concerns from Killer Phrases.

Journey to the future. Work with colleagues to visualize the future by showing what will happen if you do implement the idea – and what will happen if you don't.

LEADERSHIP ACTION

Replace "It's not in the budget" with:

Can we fund a prototype or a test?
Can we borrow the money from other sources or pool budgets?
How can we enact our plan for free?

STALLS

Our cartoons will never be sold on videotape. — *Disney corporate policy, mid-1970s*

"I've never given anything away in my life, and I'm not about to start now."
— *John D. MacArthur, whose posthumous billion-dollar foundation endows creative endeavors*

"When in danger or in doubt – run in circles, scream and shout." — *Navy axiom*

Sometime. Next time. Soon. Later. Sooner or later, your great ideas will encounter the Staller – the naysayer with an iron will and a Jell-O spine. Sure, new ideas benefit from additional input. But, the Staller is an expert in the art of energetic non-action.

"Putting it through channels" spells defeat in today's market. To survive, organizations must advance with straightforward speed and simplicity. What GE calls getting that small-company soul inside a big-company body.

Although we tend to envision stalls as "stone walls" of resistance, the best Stallers devise mudholes and quagmires. The Staller's uniquely circular goal is to slow you down, to buy time, to keep your idea in limbo until it no longer poses a threat.

Your mission is to uncover the perceived threat – and get your idea back on solid ground.

> **"Old Truth:
> Haste makes waste.**
>
> **New Truth:
> Thoughtful speed
> improves quality."**
>
> — *Motorola, Inc.*

THE BIRTH OF PATENT *PENDING*

PUT IT IN WRITING.

The first date of Killer Phrases. You have to show your stuff and then wait by the phone until "they" condescend to call. This gives you plenty of time to think the worst, especially if they forget....

> a/k/a: *Put it through channels.*
> *Fill out this form.*
> *Mail us your resume.*

Sending your new idea off by itself can leave you feeling exposed and helpless. Besides packing your idea a nice lunch, here are some things you can do:

Get on the same wavelength. Schedule a five-to ten-minute briefing session before you write anything. Define mutual criteria for the success of your idea.

Make it reader-friendly. Double spacing with wide margins leaves room for editorial comments and buy-in. Include a cover note offering to discuss ideas and answer questions.

Clarify next steps. If you haven't heard by the agreed-upon date, what can you do to close the loop?

LEADERSHIP ACTION

Show that "Put it in writing" does not spell Killer Phrase in your organization. Set clear guidelines for submitting ideas, formally and informally. Focus on rapid turnaround and specific feedback.

Join leaders like Toyota whose Creative Idea Suggestion System has generated over 20 million ideas in 40 years, with more than 90% accepted. Toyota's GI (Good Idea) Club helps orient new hires to the system, while managers assist as needed with anything from a feasibility test to writing tips.

> **Did you know that if we remove the official paperwork from a U.S. aircraft carrier, it will actually float two feet higher in the water?**

STALLS

YES!

a/k/a: ...stare...
...rolled eyes...
...curled mouth...
...hand covering face...

Silence is a reaction. Identify the reaction and proceed accordingly.

Silence is golden? On average, introverts take eight seconds longer to respond in conversation. They also score significantly higher than extroverts in creativity tests, which may make them more open to your idea. So, give it an extra eight seconds.

Don't assume the worst. Silence doesn't always mean "no." Perhaps your listeners simply need time to build a mental model.

Don't be afraid of silence. Nature abhors any vacuum, including silence during meetings and presentations. Anticipate the silence and let it work for you, as others attempt to fill in with their opinions.

Go off the record. Higher-ups may be wary of giving responses that sound like official endorsement. Ask for informal feedback.

"Glad you don't object." If you like to live dangerously, take silence as assent. Weigh potential wins and losses before you take this drastic step.

— a common response to new ideas

LEADERSHIP ACTION

Understand the mix of introverts and extroverts on your staff. Use pacing, pauses, advance notice, and other techniques that permit time for reflection. Allow silence. To solicit opinions, ask open-ended questions such as "What do you think?"

I'LL GET BACK TO YOU.

The hold button of Killer Phrasedom. Your great idea will be handled in sequence by the next available naysayer.

> *a/k/a:* *That's a subject for another meeting.*
> *I'm sorry...did you say something?*
> *Let's put that on the back burner.*
> *That's interesting, BUT...*

Confirm that you are on hold, not disconnected, with the appropriate line of questioning.

Clarify the reason. Find out whether this is a delay, a lack of time or a legitimate need to confer. Is there an advantage to the delay? Does the boss have to check things out?

Clarify the situation. Agree on the need for input. Explain that you can't do anything until you get it. Is there anyone else who can provide this information or is this person the single, final authority? Offer to help gather any additional information required.

LEADERSHIP ACTION

Define your reasons for the delay. Also, if you can't advance the idea, say so. Specify when you will respond. "I'll get back to you by Tuesday" is a delay, not a Killer Phrase.

GET A COMMITTEE TO **LOOK** INTO THAT.

> "[People] see what is wrong with a new thing, not what is right. To verify this...submit a new idea to a committee."
>
> — *Charles Kettering, engineer and inventor*

Like the infamous Energizer Rabbit some committees just keep going...and going...and going.

a/k/a: *Let's give it more thought.*
          Let's pull together the experts.
          Conduct a survey.

Turn bored boards and painful panels into admiring advocates.

Volunteer to help. Whether this is a stall or a legitimate request for more input, take advantage of it. The naysayer has set the stage for others to hear your idea! Offering to help select, notify or serve on the committee can facilitate both the task and your idea's acceptance.

Encourage a deadline. For the proposal...the prototype...the decision. Set milestone dates to advance your idea from committee to commitment.

LEADERSHIP ACTION

Keep committees simple. Focus on evaluating one specific problem and related solutions.

Keep committees small. Self-directed committees of three to six people produce fast turnarounds.

Keep committees deadline-driven with weekly meetings and a final presentation within about 45 days.

Creatively name your committee, such as DuPont's "Oz Group," to transform a collection of individuals into an enthusiastic team.

Empower the committee. Invite the idea proposer to serve on the committee. Avoid roadblocks and disillusionments by including a "bureaucracy buster" who can champion the process to successful completion.

ZERO DEFECTS

"Any change, at any time, for any reason is to be deplored." — *Duke of Cambridge*

"You can have any color you want, boys, as long as it's black."
— *Henry Ford, founder of Ford Motor Company*

"Who the hell wants to hear actors talk!"
— *Harry Warner, president of Warner Brothers, 1927*

"Do it right the first time." — *Total Quality Management slogan*

Perfect skin. Perfect relationship. Perfect world. "Zero Defects" makes an admirable goal but a rotten motivational slogan. We need standards, but Zero Defect naysayers want to begin at the end. Truth is, it's a dead end, often protecting more problems than it solves. The demand for instant perfection creates play-it-safe environments where no one expects serendipity and people hide their mistakes.

Face it, we humans don't always get it right the first time. But give us the freedom to fail and learn, and hang on to your hat. As Steve Jobs, inventor of Apple computers, said in *Fortune* magazine, "You never heard of the Apple I."

The crack in the Zero Defects veneer is that perfectionism and quality are not interchangeable terms. Open up a new dialogue – one of continuous improvement. You can redesign the work environment to honor fast failures, shorten development cycles, and establish a collaborative climate for your idea.

> **"No idea is born perfect. Give it a chance to grow."**
>
> — *Rapp Collins Marcoa, advertising agency*

YES!

IF IT AIN'T BROKE, DON'T FIX IT.

Or, as they say in New York City, "If it ain't broke...it's unbreakable!"

> *a/k/a:* *You can't argue with success.*
> *Leave well enough alone.*
> *If it's still working okay, why change it?*

Break the impasse with one of these strategies.

Preventive maintenance. Before the presentation, identify benefits of your breakthrough idea such as new product, new market share. Then, work with the naysayer to brainstorm advantages of breaking "it" before your competition does.

"Break" job. Engage in discontinuous thinking to make your idea even stronger. How can you achieve it in half the time or for half the cost? Can you make it paperless? What are the best and worst potential outcomes? How can you shift the odds of success in your favor?

Show and tell. Provide a quick history of new products improving things that weren't broken, such as superconductors, express delivery, compact discs, and microwave dinners. Established companies like Reynolds Metals keep products innovative and customers impressed by tinkering with success. They invented pop-top cans when most of us were satisfied with using can openers.

LEADERSHIP ACTION

Break it or the competition will. It's called competitive edge, added value. Japan's "amazement factor" moves new products like the Mazda Miata from "okay" to "wow." Their goal: build value and market share by surprising customers with unexpected, exciting features.

"...even if it 'ain't broke' today, it will be tomorrow. Today's innovations are tomorrow's antiques."

— *Robert J. Kriegel &*
Louis Patler,
If it ain't broke...BREAK IT!

DON'T ROCK THE BOAT.

What passes for good advice in a drifting lifeboat frequently sinks an organization.

> *a/k/a: Don't make waves.*
> *We're not out to change the world.*
> *Let's not step on anyone's toes.*
> *It's not in the regulations.*

Chart a course from troubled waters to clear sailing with one of these approaches.

Make it "see"-worthy. First, clarify the current situation and the cost of rocking the boat. What's at stake for whom? Then, flip to the opposite and talk about risks of not rocking the boat.

Trim the sails. GE Work-Out continuous improvement teams know that the simple question "Why are we doing this?" can chart new courses toward faster cycle time, product innovation and dramatic quality improvements. When you're stuck on a sandbar, rocking the boat becomes a survival strategy.

LEADERSHIP ACTION

Replace this "no rocking" metaphor with a new one. Borrow from Bill Gore, inventor of Gore-Tex: "You can try anything, as long as it's above the waterline." Ask the favorite question of Hewlett-Packard and Nippon Electric: "How can we do this in half the time?" Adopt DuPont's mindset that the penalty for inaction is greater than the penalty for action.

> "We are convinced that any business needs its wild ducks. And in IBM we try not to tame them."
>
> — *Thomas Watson, Jr., former IBM Chairman*

YES!

IT DOESN'T GRAB ME.

ZERO DEFECTS

YES!

Remember the story of the Ugly Duckling? Given a little time and care, awkward new ideas often grow into something beautiful.

> *a/k/a:* *It doesn't speak to me.*
> *It doesn't have any sizzle.*
> *That's too ivory tower.*
> *We need something more exciting.*
> *Where's the pizazz?*

Shift the focus from plain to powerful and help your idea take flight.

Where's the beef? "Sell the sizzle" was the old paradigm. The new paradigm is "Does it add value?" Post-it Notes didn't have any real appeal until people started using them. Consider a demonstration of your idea to show its added value.

Eye of the beholder. Look at your suggestion from other perspectives. First, brainstorm all its mundane traits. Then, flip to the opposite to see how you can turn those traits into eye-catching advantages. What group would it grab and why?

LEADERSHIP ACTION

The electric flowerpot didn't grab many people...until someone recognized its value as the Eveready Flashlight. Moral of the story: Don't let greatness slip from your grasp by discarding new ideas too quickly. The basis for an attention-grabbing idea is, first and foremost, a great idea. Give new ideas a chance to spread their wings in a prototype test or focus group.

LET ME PLAY DEVIL'S ADVOCATE.

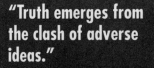

> "Truth emerges from the clash of adverse ideas."
>
> — *John Stuart Mill, philosopher*

Opposites are incredibly tempting because the grass always looks greener on the other side. But naysayers who focus on jumping from side to side rarely move ahead.

a/k/a: *That only solves half the problem.*
Think of the problems it will cause.
You haven't considered THIS.

Move from opposition to joint vision with one of these strategies.

The devil, you say. Anticipate the naysayer's desire to play devil's advocate. Invite it – after you have rehearsed your answers to likely objections.

Be devilish. Before you present, ask yourself who would not support your idea and why. What will sway opponents toward your side? During your presentation, turn adversarial win-lose discussions into win-win collaborations. Validate opposite thinking by asking "What new insights can we gain from this different perspective?"

What the devil?! Tactfully separate defensive criticism from legitimate solutions. Then, examine the solutions. Do they address this issue or a different problem?

LEADERSHIP ACTION

Avoid the temptation of equating opposite thinking with disloyalty. A wealth of innovations results from discontinuous thinking. Learn to see problems upside-down, inside-out, backwards, and from the opposite perspective. Challenge ingrained assumptions by asking, "What would we NEVER do to solve this problem?"

THE LAST PERSON WHO SAID *THAT* ISN'T HERE ANYMORE.

An epitaph to new ideas: Blessed are the trailblazers who spark innovation for they shall be fired.

> *a/k/a:* *I know someone who tried that.*
> *It doesn't fit the system.*
> *That's not consistent with the way we do things.*

Use these strategies to move from canned to can-do!

Rewrite history. You're not the person who said it before and you did your homework...right? You know your idea is good – show that this is a new situation with new outcomes.

Review the situation. Where is the "last person" now? Is that person happier? Is this an environment where people get fired for new ideas – good or bad? If so, consider looking for a new job. This may be a sign of a company in decline.

Be glad you're not the first. Often the pioneers and messengers get arrows in the back. A decade ago, casual dress at Xerox or IBM might have meant firing. Now, it's commonly accepted practice at many sites.

Are you lovesick? Have you ever seen people who are so in love with their own great ideas that they ignore valuable signals? Check the "last person's" timing and be willing to let the idea evolve slowly.

LEADERSHIP ACTION

A word to the wise: This Killer Phrase should be a warning sign. In your organization is the penalty for failure greater than the penalty for inaction? Does product-line loyalty take precedence over knowing the marketplace? Beware of missing the future and becoming a thing of the past.

> **"I don't want any yes-men around me. I want people who will tell me the truth even if it costs them their jobs."**
>
> — *Samuel Goldwyn, movie producer*

IT DOESN'T MEET OUR QUALITY STANDARDS.

This ringing catchphrase of the late '80s, designed to awaken and inspire us, is rapidly becoming the death knell for new ideas in the '90s.

> *a/k/a:* It doesn't conform to our ISO 9000 guidelines.
> Dr. Deming would never go for it.
> We'd never win the Baldrige Award with that one.
> Uh-oh, you've been to another creativity seminar.

Agree on the guidelines to save your idea from endless loops in the quality circle.

Define quality. Maybe the fact that your idea doesn't meet the current quality standards is the Good News! Show the advantages of stepping out of line, rather than forming one.

Use the right measurement. Are stated benchmarks relevant and necessary? An idea that doesn't ace the benchmarks may still move the organization in the right direction. AT&T now encourages their employees to "Do it right the SECOND time."

Give it room to grow. Today's quality standards are often noble, technically correct, and stifling. Ideas can't be expected to conform to standards right out of the chute. Show that your idea is still in the development phase, and shouldn't yet be measured by formalized criteria.

LEADERSHIP ACTION

Help teams develop an internalized passion that produces exceptional output. How? Cultivate a habit of continuous improvement that doesn't have to be measured by external standards. Influence change by fire-in-the-belly leadership, rather than rule-book management. Move into the twenty-first century with commitment and inspired action through shared, core values.

> "'Do it right the first time' programs often become ritualized, bureaucratized, spirit-destroying exercises."
>
> *— paraphrasing David Glass, CEO of Wal-Mart, in Tom Peters'* On Achieving Excellence

NO SPITBALLS   Unlearning the Rules of School

How often does voicing a new idea at work seem like being in school – raising your hand out of turn, challenging the teacher, or asking a dumb question? I believe the rules of school still plague us. "The boss will never go for it" sounds a lot like "The teacher is always right." "That isn't your responsibility" is just the grown-up version of "Keep your eyes on your own paper." And my favorite "Be realistic" reminds me of my English teacher saying "No daydreaming."

The educator John Holt said we enter school as question marks and graduate as periods. I believe we enter work as question marks and retire as periods. And maybe not raising your hand in school is equivalent to not submitting a suggestion at work.

School rarely allowed collaboration. It's no wonder that today's self-directed teams struggle. Working on teams, we want to be able to borrow, we want to pass notes, we want to all share early in the process. We don't want to always act like a relay team passing the baton from one department to another. We want to act more like a jazz group continually improvising.

So, what can we do? In your next staff meeting ask everyone to write down the rules of school that they remember. Then ask if any of those rules stifle creative thinking for your group. If so, challenge the offending rules and create new guidelines for your discussions.

> **"The difficulty lies not so much in developing new ideas as in escaping from old ones."**
>
> — *John Maynard Keynes, economist*

Old Rules of School	Guidelines for Creativity and Innovation
The teacher is always right.	Solicit opinions from those doing the work.
There's one right answer.	There are several right answers.
Keep eyes on your own paper.	Collaborate and share ideas.
Raise your hand.	Ask "What do you think" to introverts.
Grade by report cards.	Don't measure everything.
Stay on the subject.	Allow for divergent thinking.
Work alone.	Form self-directed teams.
Stop daydreaming.	Envision problems as solved and work backwards.
No spitballs.	Throw paper balls at naysayers.

Throw Spitballs?

At your next meeting, hand out a supply of scrap, reused paper. Instruct each person to wad up paper to produce an arsenal of paper balls. Then throw them at anyone who utters a Killer Phrase.

> Empowered Version: Throw ball at yourself.
> Advanced ESP Version: Throw ball before you hear it.
> Environmental Version: Save trees by using colorful Nerf balls.

You'll run a creative meeting that you will never forget!

A PARTING THOUGHT

The rules of school graduate into Killer Phrases and the impact they have on your innate creativity is devastating. Between five and seven years of age, you score higher on creativity tests than at any other time in your life. At age forty-four, you score the lowest. Fortunately, there's a magic day in your life when you start scoring higher again.

It's called retirement.

Why do we have to retire to be creative? I believe that Killer Phrases make us terminally serious. According to motivational speaker Les Brown, even 87% of our self talk is negative. "I can't... I would, but... They'll laugh at me."

Now think about the number of times per day you laugh. You laughed approximately 113 times per day as a young child, and you get down to only 11 times per day during middle age. Upon retirement – you guessed it – the laughter level goes up again.

I hope *YES,* **BUT***...* provides the strategies and laughs necessary to leap the barriers that keep you from pursuing the best solutions.

A Special Favor: *We are continually collecting new Killer Phrases and diffusing strategies. Please send or fax us your Killer Phrases, and we will mail you a free copy of our full-color Killer Phrase poster.*

Creative Management Group
226 East High Street
Charlottesville, VA 22902-5177 USA
804-296-6138 • FAX 804-979-4879

MORE KILLER PHRASES

Are you putting me on?... Because might makes right... Business is business... But, *mom*... But with the economy... CYA... Don't get me wrong... Don't give up your day job yet... Don't overload your plate... Do you think we're made of money?... Eat my shorts... Go soak your head... Have you lost your marbles?... I could care less... I don't want to hurt your feelings, but... If it doesn't work, I won't back you up... If you weren't so lazy, you wouldn't be thinking of an easier way... Is it supported by research?... It costs too much... I think you've got a brick loose... It's my way or the highway... It's not a high priority... It's too blue sky... It's too late... Let's not go off on a tangent... *MEN!*... Naah... Nobody makes a product like that... Oh, yeah, I had that idea a long time ago... Our place is too small for it... ...*RIGHT?!*... Sounds half-baked to me... Sure it will... That's some hairdo you have... That's pie in the sky... That's too hard... That time of the month?... That will screw up the works... The computer is down... The idea has to get instant results... The IRS will catch you... The old-timers won't use it... The only problem with that is... There's no community support... There you go, sticking your neck out... The women's libbers will kill you... Too academic... What a hare-brained idea... What you are really saying is... What's behind that suggestion?... When pigs fly... Who cares?... Who do you think you are?... Why start anything now?... *WOMEN!*... You can't make a silk purse out of a sow's ear... You can't save everyone... You don't know what you're talking about... You don't understand our problem... You're setting yourself up for failure...

AND THE TOP 10 FIGHT BACK PHRASES

Fight Back Phrase
(fit băk frāz) - *n.* **1. words that launch ideas into reality; usually said by achievers, leaders, and entrepreneurs. 2. the self talk of champions.**

Yes, and...
What if...?
It'll grow on you; give it a chance...
You're on the right track...
We can do a lot with that idea...
Have you considered...?
We're going to do something different today...
It doesn't have to fly...
You've sparked my interest; tell me more...
What a Great Idea!